Dwarf Caiman Crocodiles as Pets

Caring For Your Dwarf Caiman Crocodiles

Dwarf Caiman facts, care, breeding, nutritional information, tips, husbandry and more!

By Lolly Brown

Copyrights and Trademarks

All rights reserved. No part of this book may be reproduced or transformed in any form or by any means, graphic, electronic, or mechanical, including photocopying, recording, taping, or by any information storage retrieval system, without the written permission of the author.

This publication is Copyright ©2017 NRB Publishing, an imprint. Nevada. All products, graphics, publications, software and services mentioned and recommended in this publication are protected by trademarks. In such instance, all trademarks & copyright belong to the respective owners. For information consult www.NRBpublishing.com

Disclaimer and Legal Notice

This product is not legal, medical, or accounting advice and should not be interpreted in that manner. You need to do your own due-diligence to determine if the content of this product is right for you. While every attempt has been made to verify the information shared in this publication, neither the author, neither publisher, nor the affiliates assume any responsibility for errors, omissions or contrary interpretation of the subject matter herein. Any perceived slights to any specific person(s) or organization(s) are purely unintentional.

We have no control over the nature, content and availability of the web sites listed in this book. The inclusion of any web site links does not necessarily imply a recommendation or endorse the views expressed within them. We take no responsibility for, and will not be liable for, the websites being temporarily unavailable or being removed from the internet.

The accuracy and completeness of information provided herein and opinions stated herein are not guaranteed or warranted to produce any particular results, and the advice and strategies, contained herein may not be suitable for every individual. Neither the author nor the publisher shall be liable for any loss incurred as a consequence of the use and application, directly or indirectly, of any information presented in this work. This publication is designed to provide information in regard to the subject matter covered.

Neither the author nor the publisher assume any responsibility for any errors or omissions, nor do they represent or warrant that the ideas, information, actions, plans, suggestions contained in this book is in all cases accurate. It is the reader's responsibility to find advice before putting anything written in this book into practice. The information in this book is not intended to serve as legal, medical, or accounting advice.

Foreword

Dwarf Caiman Crocodilians are one of the 'smallest' versions of crocodiles out there, which is why as odd as it may seem, you can actually keep them as pets. The Dwarf Caiman's size, its exotic appearance, and its maintenance are some of the major factors on why it is attractive to potential reptile owners in general.

Keeping Dwarf Caiman as pets may be viewed as something unconventional and for some people it's dangerous. Indeed, for first time owners they could be hard to manage and maintenance can be rather difficult - that's where this book comes in. In this book you'll be easily guided on understanding your Dwarf Caiman; their behaviors, their characteristics, how you should feed and care for them and a whole lot more.

Embark on a wonderful journey of sharing your life with Dwarf Caiman Crocodilian. Learn to maximize the great privilege of living with one and be able to share this unique and unforgettable experience just like many reptile pet owners that came before you!

Table of Contents

Introduction 1
    Glossary of Reptile Terms 4
Chapter One: Getting to Know Dwarf Caimans 19
    Facts about Dwarf Caimans 20
    Different Breeds of Dwarf Caimans 23
    History of Dwarf Caimans 26
    Quick Facts 27
Chapter Two: Dwarf Caiman Requirements 29
    Legal Requirements 30
        CITES Laws for Dwarf Caiman Croc 30
    Dwarf Caimans and Other Pets 34
    Ease and Cost of Care 35
        Overall Costs 35
    Pros and Cons of Dwarf Caimans 40
Chapter Three: Tips in Buying Dwarf Caimans 43
    Where to Purchase a Dwarf Caiman? 44
    Choosing a Reputable Dwarf Caiman Breeder 48
    List of Breeders and Rescue Websites 51
    Selecting a Healthy Dwarf Caiman 54
Chapter Four: Habitat for Your Dwarf Caimans 57
    Habitat Requirements for Dwarf Caiman 58

Ideal Habitat for Dwarf Caimans 59

Cage Setup Guidelines 63

Things to Avoid Inside the Cage 65

Chapter Five: Feeding Your Dwarf Caimans 67

Nutritional Needs of Dwarf Caimans 68

Gut - load 70

Feeding Tips 74

Chapter Six: Dwarf Caiman Husbandry 77

Chapter Seven: Handling Your Dwarf Caiman 81

Basics in Handling Your Dwarf Caiman 82

Chapter Eight: 89

Breeding Your Dwarf Caiman 89

Breeding Basics 90

Nesting Baby Dwarf Caimans 92

Chapter Nine: Keeping Your Dwarf Caiman Healthy 95

Common Health Problems 96

Dwarf Caiman Care Sheet 105

Basic Information 106

Habitat Requirements 107

Nutritional Needs 108

Breeding Information 109

Index 111

Photo Credits 117
References 119

Introduction

If you're the kind of person who'd liked to try keeping wild animals or an unconventional pet that could challenge you in some way, then certainly taking care of a crocodilian could be perfect for you – particularly a Dwarf Caiman.

The Dwarf Caiman or otherwise known as *Caiman crocodilius* is the most available kind of crocodilian in pet trades. They are now quite popular as reptile pets because of its size and availability. Some species of dwarf caimans are only reserve for people who already have an experience in keeping a crocodile or small alligators, while some species can be handled easily than others. Later on in this book, we

Introduction

will discuss about the different types of Dwarf Caimans, their characteristics and if they are the type of species that is suited for you and your 'expertise.'

Before you consider getting a Dwarf Caiman as a pet, you should keep in mind that taking care of a crocodilian is something that should be taken seriously because even if they are the smallest and most popular crocodilian, the fact remains that they are still a crocodile! They can harm you and your family if you are not cautious enough. This pet is not for the weak! You have to be strong and fearless just like these creatures.

The Dwarf Caiman can be an interesting companion than the usual pets and compared to other crocodilians, they are easy to maintain in terms of costs, and housing plus they don't grow as huge as other types of crocodiles hence its name and which is why they are ideal as pets.

Before you bring a Dwarf Caiman crocodilian home, however, you should be a responsible pet reptile owner and learn everything you can about this breed and how to care of it properly. Fortunately, this ultimate guide will teach you on how to be the best Dwarf Caiman crocodilian owner you can be!

Introduction

Inside this book, you will find tons of helpful information about different types of Dwarf Caiman crocodilian; how they live, how to deal with them and realize the great benefits of owning one!

This book includes information about creating the ideal enclosures and guidelines on how to properly feed your dwarf caiman as well as tips for breeding and taking care of them. You will also find in - depth health information for the breed including common health problems affecting it and the treatment options available.

The amazing world of Dwarf Caiman crocodilian awaits! This pet is not for the faint hearted! This pet is only reserve for fearless keepers out there, are you one of them? Read on!

Introduction

Glossary of Reptile Terms

Aberrant: Deviating from the ordinary, normal or expected (Bechtel 1995).

Albundismus: A Type of Melanism in which the specimen is not completely black, but shows a change in the elements of the basic pattern as consequence of the number of isolated black spots or dots in the nonblack areas of the pattern (Peters, 1964).

Adaptation, biological: Alteration of structure or function to suit a particular environment (Bechtel, 1995).

Albino: Normal pigment is absent from the scales (Allaby, 1985). The blood pigment hemoglobin is present and may result in pinkish specimens or specimens with red eyes (Mattison, 1991). Having the absent or deficient melanin (McEachern, 1991). Widely used term for "Amelanistic".(Bechtel, 1995).

Allele: A shortening of the term allelomorph; one of two or more forms of a gene arising by mutation and occupying the same relative position (locus) on the homologous chromosome; may be distinguished by their differing effects on the phenotype (Allaby, 1985). Either of the two paired genes which affect an inheritable trait (Bechtel, 1995).

Introduction

Allophore: A cell or chromatophore containing red pigment in the skin of reptiles, amphibians, and fish (Peters, 1964; Holmes, 1979).

Amelanism: A term sometimes used instead of Amelanistic (McEachern, 1991). The appearance resulting from a lack of melanin (Barker, 2006).

Amelanistic: Having no melanin. The pigment melanin, which is responsible for black, brown, and yellow colors, is absent; specimens are pale in color, although they may have some color, especially red or pink, owing to the presence of other pigments (Mattison, 1991). A single recessive mutation resulting in a lack of black pigment referred in both skin and eyes; bright red and orange predominate (McEachern, 1991). Containing no melanin (Bechtel, 1995). The appearance created by the lack of all Eumelanin and BCM (Barker, 2006).

Amino acid: Any of the subunit building blocks that are covalently linked to form proteins (Klug, 2003). Organic compounds that are the building blocks of protein (Bechtel, 1995).

Anal scale: A single unpaired scale that covers the cloacal opening. Although it may be regarded as the posteriormost scale in the series of ventrals, the anal scale is not included in counts of the ventral scales (Barker, 2006).

Introduction

Anerythristic: Having a lack of red pigment and all red markings (Mattison, 1991). A mutation that can be caused by two separate defective genes resulting in a lack of red and orange pigment; predominantly marked with grays but also black, brown, or yellow (McEachern, 1991). An appearance that is without red; and appearance usually assumed to be the result of reduced or absent Erythrophore pigment production in the skin (Barker, 2006).

Angle of the jaw: The area on the lateral surface of the head positioned above the articulation of the upper and lower jaw bones, usually at the widest area across the head (Barker, 2006).

Anomaly: A deviation from the ordinary, normal, or expected (Bechtel, 1995).

Anterior: An anatomical direction meaning toward the front or toward the head (Barker, 2006).

Anterior prefrontals: A single pair of large plate-like prefrontals in contact with the internasals and in full contact along the midline (Barker, 2006).

Appearance: The perceived outward aspect of a snake resulting from the combination of its color and pattern. Sometimes used as a synonym of phenotype (Barker, 2006).

Arboreal: Living in trees (Bechtel, 1995).

Introduction

Axanthic: Frequently having a lack of yellow pigment; a term sometimes used instead of anerythristic, but not appropriately (McEachern, 1991). In the descriptive sense, an appearance lacking the expected visual contributions from yellow or orange pigments (Barker, 2006).

Axanthism: Literally "without yellow." The absence of yellow or orange color (Barker, 2006). Absence of yellow pigment, or absent or deficient xanthophore pigment metabolism (Bechtel, 1995).

Azygous: Occurring singly; unpaired (Barker, 2006).

Backcrossing: Mating of an organism with a parent (Bechtel, 1995).

BCM: The acronym for black cellular material, an inclusive term to refer to all the chemical compounds of black pigment found in melanophores (Nicolaus, 2001).

Bilateral: Occurring on both sides of an organism (Bechtel, 1995).

Biochrome: A pigment produced in a chromatophore (Nicolaus, 2001).

Breed true: A phenotype for a trait is said to breed true if two parents with that phenotype produce offspring of that same phenotype exclusively. In reference to a familial trait that has been reproduced through inbreeding / line breeding

Introduction

enough generations so that the offspring when bred together will produce offspring exhibiting the trait in question.

Carotene: A yellow skin pigment widely distributed in animals (Holmes, 1979). Yellow pigment (Bentley, 1982).

Carotenoids: Fat-soluble pigments widely distributed in animals and including carotene and xanthophylls (Holmes, 1979).

Carotin: Same as carotene.

Character: An observable phenotypic attribute of an organism (Klug, 2003).

Chlorophane: A green chromophane (Barker, 2006).

Chromacyte: Any cell containing a pigment (Holmes, 1979).

Chromatophores: Pigment cells (Bechtel, 1995). Cells in the skin that usually contain pigments of different colors (Bentley, 1982). A colorless body in cytoplasm and developing onto a leucoplast, chloroplast, or chromoplast (Holmes, 1979). Any cell that bears pigment and thereby plays a role in the overall color pattern of the animal (Peters, 1964).

Chromoblast: An undifferentiated pigment cell in an embryo (Barker, 2006).

Chromophane: Retinal pigment in lower vertebrates (Holmes, 1979).

Introduction

Chromosome: Each cell in every living thing has a nucleus. Much of the nucleus is made up of a constant number of paired chromosomes. Each chromosome is a single, long strand of DNA in a protein matrix. The strand of DNA contains many genes.

Chromosome: Occurring in the nucleus of a cell (Allaby, 1985). Composed mainly of DNA and basic protein, and bearing the genes being arranged in linear order (Holmes, 1979). Chromosomes are arranged in pairs with the genes being arranged on the chromosome (Mattison, 1991). The presence of homologous chromosomes is referred to as the diploid state (Allaby, 1991). Nuclear inclusion containing genes arranged in linear sequence (Bechtel, 1995).

Circumoculars: The series of scales that rim the eye, including the preoculars, a single supracular, the postoculars, suboculars, and supralabials (Barker, 2006).

Cloaca: The common chamber in the body of reptiles and amphibians into which the reproductive, intestinal, and urinary ducts open (Cogger, 1992). The external opening of the cloaca is termed the vent, anus, or cloacal opening (Barker, 2006).

Cloacae: Plural of cloaca (Barker, 2006).

Cloacal opening: The external opening of the cloaca; also termed the vent, or anus (Barker, 2006).

Introduction

Co-dominant: A gene that causes the homozygous form to look different than the wild-type and the heterozygous form to have traits of both. Some examples of this would be the Pastel, Woma Tiger, Yellow Belly, Mojave, Red Axanthic, Platinum, Butter, Cinnamon, Fire, Calico and Spot nose Ball Pythons.

Crossing over: The exchange of chromosomal material (parts of chromosomal arms) between homologous chromosomes by breakage and reunion. The exchange of material between nonsister chromatids during meiosis is the basis of genetic recombination (Klug, 2003). During meiosis, the breaking of one material and one paternal chromosome, resulting in the exchange of corresponding sections of DNA and the rejoining of the chromosome. This process can result in the exchange of alleles between chromosomes (Hartwell, 2004). Compare recombination.

Cysteine: A nonessential amino acid (meaning that the body can synthesis it) important in the synthesis of pheomelanin (Barker, 2006).

DNA (Deoxyribonucleic Acid): Molecules bearing genetic information of all living cells. Gene. Also referred to as "unit of inheritance." A molecule containing the genetic information of all living cells (Bechtel, 1995). A macromolecule usually consisting of antiparallel polynucleotide chains held together by hydrogen bonds, in

Introduction

which the sugar residues are deoxyribose. The primary carrier of genetic information (Klug, 2003). The molecule of heredity that encodes genetic information (Hartwell, 2004).

Designer appearance: Popular term referring to the phenotype resulting from the selectivebreeding to combine two or more appearances, each caused by a different mutation (Barker, 2006). See hybrid.

Dihybrid cross: Mating of individuals heterozygous for two separate inherited traits

Dimorphism: Occurrence of two forms, distinct in color or other characteristic, among animals of the same species.

Diploid: Having two sets of chromosomes; the typical zygote arrangement of chromosomes(Holmes, 1979). An individual with two chromosome sets in each cell, excluding the sexchromosome (Allaby, 1985). See haploid.

Dominance series: Dominance relations of all possible pairs of alleles are arranged in order from most dominant to most recessive (Hartwell, 2004).

Dominant: A gene that causes an animal to look different than the wild-type and where the homozygous form and the heterozygous form look the same as each other. A simple example of this would be
the Spider, Pinstripe and Granite Ball Pythons. The normal form of the gene that is usually denoted by an uppercase

symbol (McEachern, 1991). An allele that determines the phenotype of the heterozygote (Lincoln, 1990). An allele that can determine the phenotype whether heterozygous or homozygous (Bechtel, 1995).

Dominant negative : Mechanism of dominance in which some alleles of genes encode subunits of multimers that block the activity of the sub units produced by wild type alleles (Hartwell, 2004).

Dominant suppression: A form of epistasis in which a dominant allele at one locus suppresses the effect of a dominant allele at another locus (Klug, 2003).

Dopa: 3, 4-dihydroxy-L-phenylalanine, an intermediate chemical in the synthesis of melanin (Bechtel, 1995).

Dorsal: Pertaining to the back; an anatomical direction meaning toward the back (Barker, 2006). The top, back, or uppermost surface of an organism (Bechtel, 1995).

Dorsolateral: Pertaining to the area between the dorsal and lateral surfaces (Barker, 2006).

Dorsum: The upper surface or back of a python (Barker, 2006).

Double Heterozygous: being heterozygous for two different traits.

Introduction

Ectopic expression: Gene expression that occurs out side the cell or tissue where the gene is normally expressed (Hartwell, 2004).

Ectothermic (Poikilothermic or cold-blooded): Possessing no internal means for controlling body temperature (Bechtel, 1995).

Embryo: Organism in early stages of development, before it is physiologically independent (Bechtel, 1995).

Endothermic (Homeothermic or warm-blooded): Having ability to maintain constant body temperature in different ambient temperatures (Bechtel, 1995).

Epistasis: The situation occurring when one allele of one gene obliterates the phenotypic expression of all other allelic alternatives of another gene (Suzuki, et al., 1986). A gene interaction in which the affects of an allele at one gene hide the effect of alleles at another gene (Hartwell, 2004). Nonreciprocal interaction between genes such that one gene interferes with or prevents the expression of another gene (Klug, 2003).

Erythrism: Having red skin and scales caused by a lack of black pigments (eumelanin), which allows the red pigment (pheomelanin) to dominate the color of the appearance (Allaby, 1991). Abnormal or excessive amount of red coloring (Holmes, 1979). The occurrence of unusual amounts of redness in an individual or population as compared to the normal pattern of the species (Peters, 1964).

Erythrochromism: See erythrism.

Erythrocystic: See erythrism.

Erythrophores: Reddish-purple pigment-bearing cells (Holmes, 1979). Cells containing carotenes or yellow pigment(Bentley, 1982). Xanthophores that appear red (Bechtel, 1985).

Erythrophore: Red chromatophore (Bechtel, 1985).

Eumelanin: A form of melanin that is black or dark brown (Mattison, 1986). Black or brown melanin (Bechtel, 1985). See phaeomelanin.

Triple Heterozygous: Heterozygous at three gene loci.

P generation: Two unlike individuals that begin a genetics experiment, or breeding program.

F_1 **generation:** First filial generation; the offspring of the P generation. An F_1 is a single member of the F_1 generation.
F_2 **generation:** Second filial generation; the offspring of two F_1s.
F_3 **generation:** Third filial generation; the offspring of two F_2s.

Introduction

Gene: Unit of heredity that determines the characteristics of the offspring.

Genetics: The study of heredity.

Genotype: An organism's genetic composition. Heredity - the transmission of genetic characters from parents to offspring.

Het: An abbreviation for heterozygous.

Heterozygous: Possessing two different genes for a given trait. An animal with one mutated, recessive gene still appears normal; its mutated gene can be inherited by future offspring. A co-dominant animal is heterozygous for the dominant form of its mutated gene, yet is different in appearance than both the wild-type and homozygous forms.

Homozygous: A state in which both genes for a specific trait are the same. When a recessive gene is it its homozygous form, it makes the animal look different from the wild-type. When a dominant gene is in its homozygous state, it causes the animal to look different from both the wild-type and the heterozygous (co-dominant) forms.

Hypomelanistic: An animal having less black and/or brown color than a wild-type.

Leucistic: A pure white animal with dark eyes.

Introduction

Locus: A gene's position on a chromosome (plural: loci)

Melanin: Black or brown skin pigments.

Melanistic: Abnormally dark, especially due to an increase of melanin.

Mutation: An abnormal gene that under certain circumstances can cause an animal to be born with an appearance other than wild-type.

Normal: An animal with no mutated genes - "wild type" in appearance. (See wild type)

Phenotype: An animal's external appearance, as caused by its genotype.

Possible Het: An animal from a known breeding that has either a 50% or 66% possibility of being "heterozygous" for a mutant gene.

A **66% possible het** comes from breeding 2 heterozygous animals together: 50% of the offspring are heterozygous, 25% will be homozygous, and 25% will be wild-type. Of the normal appearing animals, 66% (or roughly 2 out of 3) will actually be heterozygous for the mutated gene.

A **50% possible het** comes from breeding a heterozygous animal to a wild-type animal. All of the resulting offspring

Introduction

will be wild-type in appearance, but 50% of them will actually be heterozygous for the mutated gene and must be bred out to determine which animals are really hets.

Punnett Square: A learning tool for determining the possible outcomes of a given cross between individuals. It was developed by R.C. Punnett, an early British geneticist.

Recessive: A gene that affects an animal's appearance if it's present in the homozygous state. A heterozygous animal carrying a mutated, recessive gene looks normal. Some examples of this would be Albino, Ghost/Hypo, Caramel Albino, Axanthic, Piebald, Clown, Desert Ghost, Orange Ghost, Hypo, Genetic Stripe andLavender Albino Ball Pythons.

Super: A Commonly used Herpetocultural term for the Dominant form of a Co-dominant mutation, I.E. Super Pastel.

Tyrosinase: An enzyme required for synthesizing melanin.

Tyrosinase-negative: An albino whose cells lack tyrosinase, producing a white and yellow/orange animal with pink eyes. A separate albino mutation from tyrosinase-positive. Also called T- .

Introduction

Tyrosinase-positive: An albino not able to synthesize melanin, but capable of synthesizing tyrosinase, which results in lavender-brown skin color. Also referred to as T+.

Wild-type: The way the animal usually looks in nature (i.e. the normal color and pattern).

Xanthic : Having more yellow color than wild-type.

Chapter One: Getting to Know Dwarf Caimans

Dwarf Caiman crocodilians may often times look like a really scary creature that will make you have goose bumps and be in an 'alert mode' once you see them. In whatever attitude or mood it appeals, you can expect as something that will definitely pique your interest and make you tougher and more courageous. After all only fearless people will acquire an interesting and exotic kind of pet!

Dwarf caimans may be relatively small and handy compare to taking care of a huge crocodile. But it may not be the right choice for everyone. Before you decide whether or not it might be the right pet for you and your family, you need to learn and invest a significant amount of time in

Chapter One: Getting to Know Dwarf Caimans

getting to know these creatures because it may not be suitable for first time crocodilian or reptile owners; this breed has additional husbandry requirements which may be difficult if you haven't had any experience of handling a crocodilian before.

In this chapter you will receive an introduction to the Dwarf Caiman breed including some basic facts, different types info, as well as how to deal with them. This information, in combination with the practical information about keeping reptiles in the next chapter, will help you decide if this is the perfect pet companion for you.

Facts about Dwarf Caimans

In this section you'll find some interesting fun facts about Dwarf Caiman crocodilians, their breed origin, body features, breed types and other relevant information.

The Dwarf Caiman's scientific name is *Paleosuchus Trigonatus*. It is mostly found in South America particularly in the Amazon River.

The Dwarf Caiman species can be found in and around cold streams as well as rivers or ponds. It is also found in waterfalls or rapids or bodies of water that is fast flowing – so better be careful if in case you are going on a

Chapter One: Getting to Know Dwarf Caimans

trip in an unknown falls because they love staying in cold waters compare to other crocodilians!

The Dwarf Caiman is the smallest crocodilian in the world. This specie only grows from about 4 to 6 feet; the smallest species of dwarf caiman is called the Caveas Dwarf Caiman which only grows about 4 to 41/2 feet once it reaches adulthood. Unlike most crocodilians that have yellow eye coloring, Dwarf Caimans are known to have brown eyes. This particular breed have osteoderms or bone plates, compared to other crocodile species theirs is quite huge and they have more. Their feet is also different because they have no webbing or it's not a webbed feet just like most reptiles or crocodiles for that matter. This only means that when they become adults they like to live in land or they developed into terrestrial creatures, most of them can be found in higher uplands in the wild.

In crocodilians particularly for Dwarf Caimans, the sex of the species is determined by temperature where the eggs are incubated. Incubation time of this particular species is longer than most crocodilians. They usually lay in clutches of ten to twenty eggs – if you choose to breed them (which we will tackle on in Chapter 8 of this book), expect to have lots of baby crocs around! It takes about 100 – 115 days to incubate. The female dwarf caimans have a very interesting way in how they build their nests. They build it out of decaying vegetation, and they actually lay their nests next to

Chapter One: Getting to Know Dwarf Caimans

termite mounds. Apparently, the mounds provide heat generation for the next, sometimes they'll even build on an old nest site even if the termite nest is dead (yes, it sounds gross and weird but that's how mother nature designed it). The heat from the decaying vegetation in the nest is sufficient to incubate the eggs properly. This is the only species of crocodilian that nests around termites in this particular way. This kind of behavior may help compensate for the lack of heat from the sunlight since these creatures live in shady forest habitats in the wild.

Dwarf Caimans in the wild feeds on birds, fish, reptiles and even large mammals (so better be careful – these creatures will not consider you a caretaker, to them you are just a large mammal that they could eat if you are not cautious!).

Just like any reptiles, handling dwarf caimans can be quite difficult because they will always feel threatened. It is a natural instinct to become threaten because in the wild, it only means that if somebody touches you, you're certainly a prey. If you start touching your dwarf caimans while it's still young, it may get used to you, and could be calmer compared to them being handled for the first time. Although, it's not advisable to constantly touch or handle them because it could cause stress which could also lead to illnesses.

Chapter One: Getting to Know Dwarf Caimans

Crocodilians are healthy in general but it doesn't mean that they won't get sick. Like other animals, they are also predispose to certain illnesses such as parasites, hypoglycemia, and could also suffer from different kinds of stress such as thermal stress, capture stress or social stress (which we will tackle on Chapter 9).

Different Breeds of Dwarf Caimans

In this section, you will learn the different breeds of Dwarf Caimans – their physical characteristics, their temperaments and other important details you need to consider before acquiring them. Not all of the breeds listed below are suitable for you and some may also not be available in your area, so be sure to read the common facts and also try doing a bit of research if you have selected a pet crocodilian breed. Some dwarf caimans are still rare at the time of this writing, you'd be lucky if you can find a variety of these breed in your location.

Caiman Crocodiles are a large family and it consists of many species including the dwarf caimans. There are only 2 species under the *Paleosuchus* genus: the popular Cuvier's Dwarf Caiman and Schneider's Dwarf Caiman. Many people choose the Cuvier's because it is widely available compared to the Smooth – Fronted Caiman.

Chapter One: Getting to Know Dwarf Caimans

Cuvier's Dwarf Caiman

Scientific Name: *Paleosuchus palpebrosus*

Description:

- It is classified as the smallest crocodilian species; adult Cuvier's Dwarf Caiman only reach at a maximum of 5 feet.
- It is the most preferred specie for captivity since this type of dwarf caiman is small compared to other adult crocodilians.
- It's a kind of crocodilian that doesn't enjoy being out in public, so don't expect it to be 'showy' when you put it in its cage.
- In the wild, these creatures stay in burrows most of the day; they are nocturnal which means that they only comes out during night time to foraging grounds.
- Many of these creatures can be found in single or in pairs usually in moving currents like turbid streams.
- Many pet owners found out that Cuvier's Dwarf Caiman thrives with small quantity of water compared to other crocodilian species.
- These creatures are also defecating on land (which makes it easier for you as a potential owner to clean their enclosure).

Chapter One: Getting to Know Dwarf Caimans

- This dwarf caiman is most of the time shy but can be aggressive if threatened or if they are fighting with similar captive bred crocodilians over their territory.

Range: Can be found in South America

Schneider's Dwarf Caiman or Smooth – Fronted Caiman

Scientific Name: *Paleosuchus trigonatus*

Description:

- It is relatively larger than Cuvier's Dwarf Caiman. The adult size can reach in about 5.5 to 8 feet or sometimes longer.
- It is quite harder to purchase and it is not very common in pet trade.
- The Schneider's Dwarf Caiman is very aggressive compare to Cuvier's which is why it is not as popular as a pet.
- Some species of caimans are farmed for their skin; fortunately for Schneider's Dwarf Caiman it has a smooth – fronted skin which makes it worthless for skinning.

Range: Also abundant in South America

Chapter One: Getting to Know Dwarf Caimans

History of Dwarf Caimans

We all know that crocodiles or other reptiles like alligators and lizards are descendants of dinosaurs, particularly the *crocodylomorphs* species. The *crocodylomorphs* species are the only species that survived during the Jurassic period. It later formed into different sub – species, one of which is the *eusuchians* that appeared 80 million years ago! They are the ancestors of the crocodilians that we have today.

Nobody has any extensive knowledge on how to take care of these creatures – only scientists, vets or a wild life expert can probably take care of it, and breed them properly back then. Fortunately today, because of modernization in technology and the internet, people eventually became interested in keeping these exotic creatures as pets. Several books and resources have become widely available for those who wanted to own one. Advanced keepers have dedicated in providing how – to guides about caring for a crocodilian. The knowledge about these reptiles in the last few years has blossomed and continues to expand thanks to the internet.

Today, the captive breed dwarf caimans have a stable population and it is widely available in many states, it is still not as popular as ever since it is really not a common pet but

Chapter One: Getting to Know Dwarf Caimans

many people are now becoming interested in taking care of these cool reptiles.

Quick Facts

Pedigree: evolved from archosaurs during the Triassic period

Breed Size: very small and has a relatively elongated body structure similar to a crocodile or an alligator

Length: adult length: 4 to 6 feet; smallest possible size: 4 to 4 1/2 feet

Weight: around 6 to 7 kg or 13 to 15 pounds

Coat Texture: osteoderms, can also be smooth skinned, has thick and rough scales

Color: It has various shades of green, brown, yellow, blackish, fatigue color.

Patterns/Markings: It has various patterns resembling its natural habitat

Feet Type: birds, fish, reptiles and even large mammals

Temperament: shy, aggressive, quite dangerous

Chapter One: Getting to Know Dwarf Caimans

Strangers: may be threatened around strangers or if being handled too much.

Other Pets: Not advisable to introduce to neither other house pets nor the same breed. Keeping dwarf caimans in one enclosure is not a good idea.

Training: cannot be trained, but behavior can be quite predicted if the handler already has an experience

Exercise Needs: doesn't need exercise; recommended as an observation pet only

Health Conditions: generally healthy but predisposed to common illnesses such as parasites, hypoglycemia, and could also suffer from different kinds of stress such as thermal stress, capture stress or social stress

Lifespan: average 30 to 40 years

Chapter Two: Dwarf Caiman Requirements

Interested in owning a Dwarf Caiman Crocodilian? Are you sure? If so, wow then you're one of the 'chosen' ones! It is imperative that you see the maintenance costs before acquiring it as a pet as well as the laws involved before actually deciding to buy one.

In this chapter, you will get a whole lot of information on its pros and cons, its average associated costs as well as the laws you need to be aware of so that you will be well on your way to becoming a legitimate Dwarf Caiman Crocodilian pet owner. Make sure to read this chapter because it's a pre-requisite to everything about keeping a croc!

Chapter Two: Dwarf Caiman Requirements

Legal Requirements

If you are planning to acquire a Dwarf Caiman crocodilian as your pet, there are certain restrictions and regulations that you need to be aware of. Legal requirements for keeping croc species may vary in different countries, regions, and states. It's highly recommended that you consult first with legal authorities near your area if you can or do a research online or locally.

In this section, we will provide you with an overview of the laws concerning Dwarf Caiman crocodilian in general.

CITES Laws for Dwarf Caiman Croc

The Convention on International Trade in Endangered Species (CITES) for wild fauna and flora are the governing body that is responsible in taking care of all animal species especially the endangered ones. Almost all countries in major continents all over the world are a member of CITES including USA, Europe, Latin America, Asia and Australia. It is highly recommended that you have legal or proper documents regarding any animal or species you keep as pets to save you in case of any trouble.

Chapter Two: Dwarf Caiman Requirements

CITES has 3 appendices, and each appendix contains a list of different species in different categories, and therefore has different rules when it comes to keeping, exporting and trading.

Crocodilians such as the Dwarf Caiman fall under the CITES II appendix. CITES II includes species that can be traded freely but cannot be taken from the wild.

Laws for Keeping Dwarf Caiman in the U.K.

In the UK, if you don't have the appropriate permits then you can't keep a crocodilian, it will simply be considered illegal for obvious reasons. The good news is that you can obtain permits provided that you prove to your local council that you can handle such creature, you must at least have a prior experience in taking care of this kind of reptiles and you also have to show them where you are going to keep your dwarf caiman to make sure that you meet the appropriate husbandry requirements. The enclosure must be safe and secure to prevent the animal from escaping or harming anyone.

After you've proven your 'worthiness' as a dwarf caiman keeper, the last step is to pay a fee to acquire a permit which must be renewed annually. You should also let your pet be examined by a qualified vet at least every year.

Chapter Two: Dwarf Caiman Requirements

Laws for Keeping Dwarf Caiman in the U.S.

In the United States, the laws vary from one state to another. It is highly illegal to sell crocs but it is legal to keep them, however, you have to make sure that you check first with your local authorities regarding the laws in keeping a dwarf caiman as a pet. In some states like California, they are very strict and authorities highly discouraged keeping such animals as pets, in other states they are allow keep crocodilian species provided that you have special permits since these animals are classified as dangerous creatures. Sometimes the city or county statute that prohibits keeping a dwarf caiman or any other crocodilian species supersedes some state regulations. In general, you should have documents to prove that you legally own a dwarf caiman.

The paperwork doesn't require any approval from wildlife authorities or organizations; you just need to simply provide a document stating the name, identity of the species or your dwarf caiman as well as the name address, contact details and signature of the previous owner or establishment where you bought it from. You need to also provide your own personal details and signature. This document needs to be kept for future reference if in case authorities check your legality of keeping a dangerous species as a pet.

Chapter Two: Dwarf Caiman Requirements

Conservation Concerns and Legal Documents

Some crocodilians are quite endangered already, conserving these species are a major topic and concern among wildlife enthusiasts. Dwarf Caiman breeders and pet owners believe that it is an owner's responsibility to take care of these creatures and preserve its species. All the crocodilian species including the Dwarf Caiman are all protected under international laws and these laws should be abide to ensure the stability of the species' population.

Like any other animal species such as birds, snakes or common pets like dogs and cats, illegal pet trading is a big problem because it has a huge impact in conservation issues. If you don't have the time, expertise, and money to take care of these endangered and quite dangerous creatures, it may be better to turn them over to experts or wildlife authorities. The crocs you will catch in the wild or near your area needs to be raised properly.

Chapter Two: Dwarf Caiman Requirements

Dwarf Caimans and Other Pets

It is not recommended that you introduce your dwarf caiman with other reptiles or common household pets for that matter. Dwarf caimans and crocodilians in general are dangerous animals, and they are cannibalistic. They will regard any living thing as food – yes that includes your finger! Never put another reptile, amphibian or smaller mammals inside the same enclosure because they will eat it! It is also not advisable to keep the same crocodilian breed because even if they are the same size or the same species they'll most likely compete for food or territory which could end up in a bloody ending.

There were some reports that dwarf caimans get along with turtles, you can try this if you think the turtle is large enough or too big to fit inside the mouth of your crocodilian. If your turtle are still young or small, crocs can easily cracked its shell. Be cautious if you want to introduce other breeds or even similar breeds, and make sure that the space is large enough to accommodate both of them and avoid competition.

Exposing them to strangers or other pets or constantly handling them may also affect their health and behavior because it can cause them stress which could lead to certain diseases or may even shorten their lives.

Chapter Two: Dwarf Caiman Requirements

Ease and Cost of Care

Even if these creatures are relatively small and manageable, owning and maintaining one still doesn't come cheap! The fact is that dwarf caiman crocs require maintenance which means that you have to provide supplies and be able to cover the expenses in order for you to maintain a healthy lifestyle and environment for your pet.

These things will definitely add up to your daily budget, and the cost will vary depending on where you purchase it; the brand of the materials, the nutrients included in its food and the time being. If you want to seriously own a dwarf caiman as a pet you should be able to cover the necessary costs it entails.

In this section you will receive an overview of the expenses associated with purchasing and keeping a dwarf caiman crocodilian such as its vivarium, supplements, lighting, watering and veterinary care. You will receive an overview of these costs as well as an estimate for each in the following pages of this section.

Overall Costs

The overall costs for keeping a dwarf caiman include those costs that you must cover before you can bring your

Chapter Two: Dwarf Caiman Requirements

crocodilian home. Some of the costs you will need to cover include the enclosure or cage, food and water equipment, supplies and cage décor or accessories, breeding materials, medical care - not to mention the cost of the dwarf caiman itself. It is highly recommended that you buy from legit breeders as well as during any reptile conventions or even find vivarium equipment in hardware or fixture stores because the products and materials are a lot cheaper than if you purchase everything from a pet store.

You will find an overview of each of these costs as well as an estimate for each below:

Purchase Price: $120 - $350

The cost to purchase a dwarf caiman can vary greatly depending on the breed, its age, the size of the species, genetic color and the abundance or availability in your local area. You can buy from private breeders for a much cheaper price compared to dwarf caimans being offered in pet stores. Generally speaking, pet-quality Cuvier's dwarf caiman (hatchlings and juveniles) sells for $120 to $250, while Schneider's dwarf caiman is around $200 to $350. Buying from legit breeders during a reptile convention may neither be cheap nor expensive. Keep in mind that the purchase cost is just one of the investments you need to make if you want to take care of a dwarf caiman crocodilian.

Chapter Two: Dwarf Caiman Requirements

Enclosures: $50 - $300 (depending on the current size of your crocodilian)

When you purchase a dwarf caiman you need to make sure that its vivarium or terrarium are somewhat similar to its natural habitat in the wild, so that it won't have trouble adjusting to its new environment. Providing adequate shelter will make them feel at ease and comfortable as a house pet. They may need to get used to you or other people checking them out while they are inside their enclosure so make sure that the kind of cage you will buy will protect them from any dangerous threats around the house including your house pets (perhaps it's the other way around).

Terrariums even though it may be quite time consuming in terms of cleaning it, is much suitable for your dwarf caiman because it will provide ample air circulation than aquariums. Many owners use thick glass enclosures, to prevent the animal from easily escaping. You can also opt to create a D-I-Y or Do – it – Yourself cage using alternative materials like wood; it could be a great alternative if you would want to have a cheaper enclosure.

Lighting and Gauges: $50 - $100

Adequate lighting will provide appropriate heat temperature inside your dwarf caiman's terrarium or cage

Chapter Two: Dwarf Caiman Requirements

enclosure. You need to purchase things like a UVB bulb, heat bulb and light fixtures as well. Gauges are also helpful to easily control temperatures and the cage's humidity levels.

Food and Supplements: approx.: $100

Aside from buying food like live rodents, fishes, crickets, beef and other gut loading foods you need to also provide supplements for your dwarf caiman, serves as vitamins to protect them against diseases and strengthen their body.

Veterinarian Consultations: $100 - $200

Like humans, or any other pets, crocs also get sick once in a while sometimes due to the stress in its environment. Just make sure to save up for its medical needs and vet costs. You may also need to do some medical checkups and/or lab tests once in a while for your pet or prior to you keeping it for legal purposes.

Supplies/Accessories: average of $100

In addition to purchasing your dwarf caiman's enclosure, you also need to install fixtures such as water

Chapter Two: Dwarf Caiman Requirements

filters, air heaters, lighting thermometers, water heaters, substrate and catch pole.

You should also purchase cage decors such as branches, leaves, live plants and other accessories to ensure that they'll live in a familiar habitat. The cost for these items will vary depending on the quality and also quantity, so you should budget about $100 or more for these extra costs.

Expenses Overview

Needs	Costs
Purchase Price	$120 - $350 (£93.06 - £271.43)
Enclosures	$50 - $300 (£38.77 - £232.65)
Lighting and Gauges	$50 - $100 (£38.77 - £77.55)
Food and Supplements	$100 (£77.55)
Vet Consultations	$100 to $200 (£77.55 - £155.10)
Supplies/Accessories	$100 (£77.55)
Total	$520 to $1,150 (£403.26 – £891.82)

*Costs may vary depending on location
**Costs may change based on the currency exchange

Chapter Two: Dwarf Caiman Requirements

Pros and Cons of Dwarf Caimans

Before you bring a dwarf caiman home you should take the time to learn the pros and cons of the breed. Every crocodilian breed is different so you need to think about the details to determine whether a dwarf caiman is actually the right pet for you.

In this section you will find a list of pros and cons for dwarf caiman crocodilian specie:

Pros for Dwarf Caiman Crocodilian:

- A pet that doesn't need to interact constantly with owners
- A pet that is satisfied and happy inside its enclosure or terrarium
- A pet that has the ability to easily adapt to its environment
- A pet that doesn't require exercises or training
- A pet that doesn't require being handled too much
- A pet that has no special needs unlike popular or high – energy pets that demands attention.
- A pet that has a long lifespan
- A pet that is interesting and also challenging

Chapter Two: Dwarf Caiman Requirements

Cons for Dwarf Caiman Crocodilian:

- A pet that can be quite dangerous
- A pet that is not for newbies or untrained reptile keepers
- May come across as boring or non – interactive
- Cannot be handled all the time
- Quite sensitive and dangerous
- Not advisable in keeping with other pets
- Can be quite expensive in terms of its habitat needs or maintenance

Chapter Two: Dwarf Caiman Requirements

Chapter Three: Tips in Buying Dwarf Caimans

Now that you are already aware and have prior knowledge about the legal aspects of owning and maintaining a Dwarf Caiman croc as well as its pros and cons, the next step is purchasing one through a legitimate breeder or during reptile conventions. In this chapter you will find valuable information about where to find a Dwarf Caiman crocodilian breeder, how to quarantine them, and how to differentiate a healthy dwarf caiman from an unhealthy one.

Chapter Three: Tips in Buying Dwarf Caimans

Where to Purchase a Dwarf Caiman?

It is best that you purchase a captive bred dwarf caiman from legit breeders. You can actually purchase from several sources such as specialist pet stores (although it might be a bit more expensive), private breeders (make sure they have proper documents), breeders recommended by hobbyist reptile magazines, reptile conventions as well as your local herpetological society. There are a lot of dwarf caiman collections in herp societies because this is where dwarf caiman's usually ends up once their owners gets bored with them or could not take care of them for some reason.

It may cost you a little extra dollars but it is worth it because you will be assured that your dwarf caiman is healthy and doesn't have any illnesses or transmitted diseases unlike if you are going to just purchase from backyard or unknown breeders. Aside from that it will also benefit captive breeding programs, and will help them to further breed healthy caimans in the future.

If you choose to buy from a backyard breeder, you may not be certain about its health, and these dwarf caimans that are caught in the wild may be endangered already. You may risk from the issues of importation damages – these are

Chapter Three: Tips in Buying Dwarf Caimans

animals that are illegally imported from the wild every year and are usually in poor health condition.

These wild dwarf caimans may also have difficulty in adjusting to a captive life. It is also not recommended that you buy from local pet stores (you should buy from pet stores specializing in reptiles) because most of it is only selling dwarf caimans for profit and most often than not some of these creatures are in poor condition because they are living in an unhealthy environment.

The needs of dwarf caimans in general are overlooked by pet stores, and if you buy from them for the sole reason that you want to rescue the animal from an inadequate environment, the store will only replace it or re-stock it with another dwarf caimans without investing in proper care, and without improving environmental conditions, that is why it is better if you give your money to legitimate captive breeding programs.

Before purchasing you should also first identify if the dwarf caiman crocodilian is a captive breed or caught in the wild. Another important tip is to verify with the seller or provider the kind of species or the kind of dwarf caiman you are purchasing in order to make sure that you are getting the appropriate species so you can also give it the appropriate care.

Chapter Three: Tips in Buying Dwarf Caimans

If your provider is unsure then you may ask a reputable source or an expert in dwarf caiman crocs to identify the kind of breed you want to buy.

Aside from local pet stores, legitimate breeders, and reptile conventions, you can also get referrals on where you can purchase a healthy dwarf caimans from several forums online or online communities. These communities usually have contacts, has history information regarding responsible breeding, and you can also get ideas on how to properly care for your new pet croc.

Quarantine

Whether reptiles or crocodilians are caught from the wild or breed in captivity, these creatures should be quarantined for at least 45 days.

Quarantining your dwarf caimans should be strictly done in order for you to assess the health of your pet and to make sure that it is not a carrier of transmittable disease to prevent it from being transferred to you, your other pets or your family.

The main reason for this specifically for dwarf caimans is that these creatures may not show any signs of illnesses and can hold on to it for a long time without being noticed. The environmental stresses of shipping, traveling or being in a

Chapter Three: Tips in Buying Dwarf Caimans

new habitat can trigger a hidden ailment. If you do not quarantine a pet, it can expose your other pets to potentially infectious or viral diseases.

Here are some steps you need to take for a successful quarantine period for your dwarf caimans:

- Put your new dwarf caiman crocodilian in a separate room, away from your other pets or other dwarf caimans for at least 45 days.

- Make sure to feed and handle all your other pets before introducing or placing the newly quarantine crocodilian with them to avoid contamination.

- Make sure to use separate equipment for the quarantined croc, and always wash your hands after handling them.

- Cage hygiene should always be done to prevent the spread of germs or parasites. The reason for this is that new imported reptiles including dwarf caimans may have intestinal parasites. Constantly cleaning and furnishing will help avoid these problems.

Chapter Three: Tips in Buying Dwarf Caimans

- It is highly recommended that you test your new pet's fecal sample and give it to your vet for diagnosis and testing.

Choosing a Reputable Dwarf Caiman Breeder

To make sure that you get a well-bred, healthy and robust dwarf caimans, your best bet is to look around for a legitimate breeder. Feel free to ask around at the various dwarf caiman or reptile forums online so that you can get a personal recommendation from friends or your local veterinarian. Once you have your list of breeders on hand you can go through them one-by-one to narrow down your options. Below are some guidelines to help you choose a reputable dwarf caiman crocodilian breeder:

The first thing you should do is to check the legality and capability of the breeder. It's highly recommended that you visit the website for each breeder on your list or their social media page (just to see what kind of person they are). Look for essential information about the breeder's history and experience when it comes to taking care of reptiles or crocodilians for this matter. Make sure to ask and check their licenses or document registrations (they should have one because it is required by law) to ensure the legitimacy of the breeder and the legality of the animals. You can also check

Chapter Three: Tips in Buying Dwarf Caimans

or ask if he/she can provide any info about his/her facilities or the kind of place where they are breeding these animals. If they can't show it or can't provide sufficient info then you should just move on. Don't waste your time in breeders who can't even share such information, they should be open to questions like this.

The next step is to personally interview the potential breeder. Either you meet with them or communicate online or via phone. You should ask the breeder questions about his experience with breeding crocodilians in general and about the specific dwarf caiman breed you are looking for. It's also advisable that you ask for information about the breeding stock including registration and health information (if they have any). Another good sign that your potential breeder is reputable and responsible is that they too will ask you questions because they wanted to also make sure that their crocs are going to good homes and great caretakers.

Now comes the final and crucial test; after confirming and deciding your 'top' potential breeders, you should then go to their place and do an onsite inspection. You should schedule an appointment to visit the facilities and also ask for a tour including the place where the dwarf caiman collections are kept. If the surroundings look unorganized or unclean, do not purchase from the breeder or from the local pet store. Make sure the collections are in good condition

Chapter Three: Tips in Buying Dwarf Caimans

and that the dwarf caiman crocodilians are all healthy - looking and active.

Characteristics of a Reputable Dwarf Caiman Breeder

By this time you should have narrowed down the best of the best breeders on your list, before making a decision consider every factor to make the most out of it. Make sure the breeder provides some kind of health guarantee and ask about any medical information the dwarf caimans may already have. Below are some characteristics you should look out for when selecting a reputable breeder.

- The breeder should be willing to educate or explain and answer all your questions expertly.

- The breeder should allow on - site visits, however if you are far from the place, you should be able to request photos or videos from the breeder and he/she should gladly show them to you so that you won't waste your time.

- The breeder should offer a contract and some sort of warranty.

- The breeder should be willing to take back or rehome the dwarf caiman croc regardless of the situation.

Chapter Three: Tips in Buying Dwarf Caimans

- The breeder should allow you to reach him/her before and after purchasing the dwarf caiman croc.

- The breeder should be able to provide health records and also have contacts with veterinarian as well as firsthand information about the dwarf caiman's overall health.

- The breeder should also explain to you the risks or the cons of keeping one as a pet not just its advantages.

- The breeder should be transparent and honest about how they raised and bred dwarf caiman crocs so that you'll know that they're reputable and a caring owner as well.

List of Breeders and Rescue Websites

As mentioned earlier you can buy from several sources, that's why you need to do some research and decide which breed you want before you start shopping around. When you are ready to buy a dwarf caiman croc, you then need to start thinking about where you are going to get it. You may be able to find a dwarf caiman at some local breeders near your area, but think carefully before you buy whether that is

Chapter Three: Tips in Buying Dwarf Caimans

really the best option. Follow the quick guidelines mentioned earlier to ensure the quality of its breeding.

If you want a baby or juvenile dwarf caiman crocodilian, you can probably find some at rescue websites, you may also try adopting a croc from a reputable breeder as well, or purchase from the exerts at reptile convention events, who knows it might be the better option for you.

Here is the list of breeders and websites that sell dwarf caiman crocodilians:

Breeders and Rescue Websites

Back Water Reptiles
<http://www.backwaterreptiles.com/alligators/dwarf-caiman-for-sale.html>

Underground Reptiles
<https://undergroundreptiles.com/product-category/animals/lizards/crocodilian/>

Reptile Trader UK
<http://www.reptiletrader.co.uk/reptiles/RT39127>

Kingsnake (includes other reptiles)
<http://market.kingsnake.com/index.php?cat:119>

Chapter Three: Tips in Buying Dwarf Caimans

Whole Sale Exotics
<http://www.wholesaleexotics.com/reptiles/wholesale-reptiles-for-sale.html>

New England Reptile Shop
<http://www.newenglandreptileshop.com/product-category/lizards-for-sale/>

Chute Libre
<https://chutelibre.info/full-grown-dwarf-caiman>

Tap – a – Talk
<https://www.tapatalk.com/topic/585140-80296>

Urban Reptiles
<http://www.urbanreptiles.com/>

ReptilesNCritters
<http://www.reptilesncritters.com/smooth-front-caimans.html>

Caiman Hunter
<http://www.caimanhunter.com/>

Monster Fish Keepers
<https://www.monsterfishkeepers.com/forums/threads/my-dwarf-caiman.501796/>

Chapter Three: Tips in Buying Dwarf Caimans

Arrow Head Reptile Rescue
<http://www.arrowheadreptilerescue.org/intake/>

Grange Reptiles UK
<http://grangereptiles.co.uk/dwa.php>

Selecting a Healthy Dwarf Caiman

As mentioned earlier selecting a healthy crocodilian will save you from a lot of headaches and vet bills in the long run. If you are a first time dwarf caiman owner, it is best to start off with a healthy one because an ill crocodilian can be very challenging to the inexperienced. Crocs are the kind of animals that are somewhat shy and don't like to be seen a lot which is why it may also be unnoticeable if they are suffering from any kind of illness. It's imperative that before purchasing one you should look for basic signs of a healthy dwarf caiman.

After you have narrowed down your list of options to just two or three dwarf caiman breeders, your next step is to actually pick out the croc you want. You have already determined that the remaining breeders on your list are responsible, but now you need to make sure that the dwarf caiman crocs they have available are healthy and ready to go home with you.

Chapter Three: Tips in Buying Dwarf Caimans

Here are some few guidelines to keep in mind when selecting a healthy dwarf caiman crocodilian:

Signs of a Healthy Dwarf Caiman:

- The dwarf caiman should try to bite you when you handle it; it is usually a good sign because it means that they are alert. The creature should also be active and do some vocalization (reptile sounds – don't confuse it with singing!)

- Watch out for lethargic animals because they may be ill or too cold. There's a difference between being calm while still being alert and completely non – reactive at all.

- Check for any injuries if the crocs are kept together; small cuts, bites or scratches are common but they should be minor injuries.

- Make sure that the skin is clean, free from fungus or other parasites and the belly should be smooth.

- There should be no discharge in the eyes; it must be fully open and clear; should have no sign of mites around the eyes.

Chapter Three: Tips in Buying Dwarf Caimans

- There should be no discharge in its nose and its mouth should also be clean.

- Make sure to check out the back of its throat because there could be inflammation which could be a sign of respiratory problems or secondary infections.
- Its vent should be clean.

- Make sure that the earflaps are free from parasites. It's not normally a concern but if the dwarf caiman has a parasite that means they might have an illness.

- Check its tail base. It must be plump and firm, if it is not then that means the crocs are not being properly fed because the tail and the neck are where fats are being stored.

- The osteoderms or plates should not be enlarged.

- If you will be given a hatchling, makes sure that there aren't any signs of yolk scar in its belly. There should also be no excess tissue attach, its belly should be smooth.

- If the yolk sac is infected for newborns it would lead to fatality, so don't purchase them anymore.

Chapter Four: Habitat for Your Dwarf Caimans

The dwarf caiman makes an awesome pet largely because of its size, quite docile personality and its exotic qualities, although these dwarf caiman can easily adjust and adapt to a new living condition, it may still be quite challenging especially for first time crocodilian keepers. You may want to make your new pet as comfortable as it can be so that it can get used to its new home, and to also avoid being stressed out.

In this chapter you will learn the basics about your dwarf caiman's habitat requirements including on how to set up its cage, useful accessories, and some things to avoid when it comes to setting up its enclosure or terrarium.

Chapter Four: Habitat for Your Dwarf Caimans

Habitat Requirements for Dwarf Caiman

Since dwarf caimans are relatively small and don't grow very big compare to other crocodilian species, it may not need too much space to roam around with but you still have to ensure that it's adequate for them as they grow.

One of the major advantages of having this creature as a pet is their low maintenance in terms of its habitat requirements compared to larger animals or common pets such as dogs or cats. But aside from space, the main thing your dwarf caiman needs in terms of its habitat is lots of love and affection from his human companions through providing them with adequate living condition. Dwarf caimans may not be the kind of breed that bonds closely with family and they could never be a trusty companion, but just like any other pets you should make an effort to spend some quality time with your pet crocodilian each and every day. If your dwarf caiman doesn't get enough attention you may not notice if it's ill or stress.

In addition to building its habitat requirements, you also need to add other terrarium accessories not just for aesthetic purposes but mainly for the purpose of resembling the dwarf caiman's habitat or environment in the wild.

Keep reading to learn the basics about your dwarf caiman's habitat requirements. You will be given tips and

Chapter Four: Habitat for Your Dwarf Caimans

guidelines on how to create and maintain an ideal habitat for your pet crocodilian.

Ideal Habitat for Dwarf Caimans

As mentioned earlier in this book, you need to house your pet crocodilian in an enclosure or a terrarium so you can keep them safe and secure as they grow. They could be quite dangerous and they are mostly an observation kind of pet only. Never let them roam around the house unsupervised. That's not a good idea.

- **Size of Enclosure**

The rule of thumb when it comes to building or purchasing an enclosure for your dwarf caiman is that the size or space should have a land area and a water area. As mentioned on the first chapter of this book, crocodilians prefer cold streaming water, they love to swim but for other species particularly the dwarf caimans they are more terrestrial especially when they get older. Most pet owners filled the cage with water (about 70 – 80% of the space available), and then the rest of it is land or dry area, where they can bask and also walk around comfortably. It is preferred that the dry area's space be twice as long as the current size of your pet so that it can roam around with ease.

Chapter Four: Habitat for Your Dwarf Caimans

The ideal cage size according to most croc owners should be 2 x 1.2 x 1.3 metres (6'7" x 3'11" x 4'3"). For hatchlings you can buy or build a terrarium with a size of 1.2m x 0.6m x 0.6m high (3.9' x 2' x 2'). The enclosure should ideally contain 140 – 150 gallons. Of course, once your pet gets larger, you may need to replace your terrarium and put your dwarf caiman in a larger enclosure.

For dwarf caimans, experts recommend that you purchase a glass cage like an aquarium simply because it can easily be planted with branches, and you can also landscaped its bottom part to make it look like a forest floor. However, some pet owners also suggest buying a wooden terrarium as an alternative to a glass terrarium. The most important thing is that it should be sealed and secured to prevent your pet from escaping.

Dwarf Caimans may or may not successfully co - exist with each other so better not house them together because it could lead to cannibalism although there were some reports that they get along with their own breed provided that they have more than enough space and enough food.

Keep in mind though that your dwarf caiman collections should not feel stressed out by the presence of its other occupants. You should also make sure that there are lots of hiding places, lots of branches (for exercise/climbing opportunities) and lots of plants inside. These creatures are quite shy remember?

Chapter Four: Habitat for Your Dwarf Caimans

- **Gravel, Stones, Rocks and Some Plants**

We all know that dwarf caimans or crocodilians for that matter are quite shy and also enjoys being both in water and land, they are semi – aquatic creatures. In the wild, they are mostly found in rapids, streams, waterfalls, and dry land, which is why you should provide them with that kind of environment inside their enclosures. They will be spending most of their time in the water but they also need dry land for basking. You should consider the heat temperature in both the water and land area which we will tackle later on in this book.

In line with this, you should be able to provide lots of branches and plants or leaves as well as hiding places or areas for your dwarf caimans because that will enable them to practice their natural ability, make them feel comfortable in their new home, and will also make them feel close to their natural habitat even in captivity.

Try adding gravel and stones or rocks as well as green or brown leaves (fresh or fake) because it will make your dwarf caiman feel safe as if they were still living in the wild, and once they feel secure there's a chance that you can most likely see them out of their hiding places, and be able to observe them.

Chapter Four: Habitat for Your Dwarf Caimans

You can use both fake and real live plants; live plants can help increase as well as maintain humidity inside the enclosure. Another advantage of using real plants is that if ever your dwarf caiman decides to eat it, it will be edible and safe. It's highly recommended that you use real plants.

Keep in mind to only use non – toxic plants so that the feeder bugs could also eat them. If you buy a plant from the pet store you may not be sure if it is safe for your crocodilian due to insecticides and toxic fertilizers that could affect your pet just make sure to properly wash them with soap and water to remove harmful chemical residues. Keep in mind though that the plants may get knocked off by your dwarf caiman so just limit the amount of plants inside the enclosure

Make sure to also provide a hiding space in the land area near the water. Hatchlings and young dwarf caimans loves to hide and burrow themselves in. There should also be a zone in the cage used for basking for your pet to feel safe, comfortable and happy with its surroundings. Remember that a great living condition can improve your dwarf caiman's health and overall lifespan.

Chapter Four: Habitat for Your Dwarf Caimans

Cage Setup Guidelines

There are many ways on how to set up a great habitat for your dwarf caiman crocodilian, but aside from the materials used for its cage, you also need to include equipment to sustain an adequate living condition for these animals. Below are some general guidelines you should follow when installing these equipment.

- **UVB/UVA Light/ Lighting Fixtures**

Every cage or enclosure should have one UVB light as well as one UVA light. The UVB light aids in the synthesis of Vitamin D3, it acts as replacement for the sun's heat while the UVA light is known to have positive effects among reptiles including crocodilians because it could boost their immune system and make them active and alert. It's important that the lights be placed on top and it is outside the cage with the light shining downwards. The UVB light bulb must also be replaced at least every 6 months, and the heat bulb (40 – 60 watts) should also be replaced once it burns out. Your dwarf caiman will need that for basking once they are staying the dry area inside the cage.

For the lighting fixtures, you should opt to buy a linear fluorescent fixture and also a spotlight fixture used for the heat bulb. It's always available in hardware or home improvement stores. It's also highly recommended that you purchase an automatic timer for the lighting.

- **Water and Air Heaters**

Water and air heaters are needed since your pet is semi – aquatic and your enclosure has two areas. You have to make sure that there are water and heat regulators or thermostat so that you can easily adjust the water and air temperature to prevent the cage from overheating. A 300 watt water heater can heat 300 liters of water. If you use less powerful heaters it can take longer to heat the water. For air heaters, you can buy 150 watts of ceramic heat emitters. Make sure that your dwarf caiman can't reach the heaters as well as the wires because it could electrocute them or burn their skin. You can use a foil to cover the wires so that your pet won't try to chew it.

- **Screens/Top Lids and Ventilation**

There should be a screen on top of the cage simply because UVB rays cannot penetrate plastic or glass. The screen cages should also have good ventilation. You should also adjust the ventilation based on the kind of cage you purchase for your dwarf caiman.

Chapter Four: Habitat for Your Dwarf Caimans

Things to Avoid Inside the Cage

- **Waterfall**

Although dwarf caimans love waterfalls or free flowing water, it should not be used inside the cage because it harbors molds and bacteria which are not safe for drinking.

- **Water Bowl**

Obviously, dwarf caimans don't drink from water bowls. Don't try to place a bowl inside their enclosure because it will be of no use and bacterial growth could also take place plus these creatures are not or cannot ever be trained to drink out of a bowl just like cats or dogs.

- **Heat Rocks**

Dwarf caimans love to burrow themselves under rocks and soil. Using heat rocks or ground heaters can easily burn their feet and belly. Don't ever use heat pads or heat rocks or if you do, make sure that the overall temperature of the enclosure is just warm enough.

Chapter Four: Habitat for Your Dwarf Caimans

- **Light bulbs that are inside cage**

Dwarf caimans can climb and crawl that's why they can easily reach the top of their cage where most heating and lighting equipment are attached. It's important that you don't put the light bulbs or any lighting fixtures inside their cage because it can easily burn them and it's not safe.

Chapter Five: Feeding Your Dwarf Caimans

Meeting your dwarf caiman's nutritional needs is very important to ensure that your pet stays healthy, and strong against diseases. Every kind of crocodilian species have different nutritional requirements, that's why reading this chapter is important because it will focus only on dwarf caiman breed. Crocs, like many other pets, should be given the right amount of recommended food for a balanced nutrition because proper diet can also lengthen their life.

In this section, you'll learn the majority of your pet's nutritional needs; tips on how to feed them as well as recommended foods that are good for their health and foods to avoid.

Chapter Five: Feeding Your Dwarf Caimans

Nutritional Needs of Dwarf Caimans

In the wild, dwarf caiman crocodilians are opportunistic predators. They will eat various kinds of prey such as reptiles, amphibians, mammals, insects and even fresh water animals whichever is available in a particular season. For hatchlings they usually eat smaller fishes, insects and amphibians or reptiles but as they grow older they tend to eat larger preys including their own kind as well as other freshwater animals particularly crustaceans and mollusks such as crayfish and snails.

For captive bred dwarf caimans, it's actually the same type of diet, but since you are keeping them, it's your duty to make sure that they are getting a balanced nutrition. Like many animals (and humans), dwarf caimans need proper amounts of protein, carbohydrate, fibre, vitamins, and minerals. Usually, dwarf caiman crocs will eat anything you feed them, so if for example you feed a whole animal such as a rat, it's already a full meal packed with all the essentials. The protein/carbs will be coming from the meat of the rat; the calcium is from the bones etc. However, you may need to gut – load some of their foods so that they can get the right amounts of calcium because calcium – deficiency is very common among reptiles and it takes a while before you notice any signs that they are lacking in calcium. We will talk about gut – loading your dwarf caiman's food in a bit.

Chapter Five: Feeding Your Dwarf Caimans

For most owners, they feed their dwarf caimans a variety of fish as well, so that your croc can have a variety of food nutrients. Try feeding them an ocean perch or herring fishes, however, it's also important to note that if you feed frozen or live fish it could have disadvantages because fishes contain large amounts of the enzyme thiaminase which destroys Vitamin B1 (thiamine) aside from that, if you only feed your dwarf caiman a fish (especially oily fish) they could develop Vitamin E deficiency, which could lead to future problems. Feeding them occasional ocean perches, herring fishes or other kinds of fish that doesn't contain enzyme thiaminase can be best for your croc.

Aside from whole preys and fishes, you can also feed your dwarf caimans with variety of food items such as pork, chicken, beef (minced, sliced or with bones), spiders, frogs, lizards, earthworms. For hatchlings or juvenile you can feed them a variety of insects or finely chopped meat so that they can digest it easily. Compared to adult dwarf caimans, young crocodilians' digestive system are still fragile, they may not be able to break down food easily especially if you feed them insects with hard exoskeletons so it is better for you to mince these preys into small dishes to avoid stomach problems.

You can also buy pelletized food from pet stores, your dwarf caiman may not easily feed on them but when they got used it it'll be much easier for you and much safer for

Chapter Five: Feeding Your Dwarf Caimans

your pet because it will reduce the risk of unwanted parasites or diseases.

How Often Do You Need to Feed Your Dwarf Caimans?

Dwarf caimans should be fed at least thrice a week or once every two days for young crocodilians. As your pet gets older and its prey gets larger, you can reduce its feeding to twice a week to avoid overfeeding. Females who are pregnant may only eat a small amount of food because there is no more space in their abdomens. Make sure to keep an eye on their weight and their eating behavior so you can adjust your feeding schedule or the amount of food you give to them.

Gut - load

Gut loading of food is a kind of process where you increase the nutritional value of the prey that you feed to your dwarf caiman crocodilian. The concept is very simple, since we all live in an ecosystem, we all benefit from one another in various ways. A great example is the eagle, eagles eat snakes, while snakes eat rodents or chickens, chickens feed on worms, and worms feed in various sources. It is same with dwarf caimans in the wild, their wild preys also feed on many different nutrition sources within that

Chapter Five: Feeding Your Dwarf Caimans

ecosystem, which makes balance nutrition. However, in captivity, it's just impossible to create that kind of natural cycle, so in order to replicate that you as the owner should properly gut load the food that you feed your dwarf caimans.

You need to also properly feed the insects or the prey a special diet or good nutrition so that in the end your crocodilian will benefit from that very balanced and proper nutrition. In order for you to gut load the food of your dwarf caiman crocodilian you should supplement it with a multivitamin powder with calcium, it could also aid in providing your pet with the minerals and vitamins it needs.

Unfortunately, most commercial gut loads are low in calcium and minerals which may not be sufficient for your caiman's nutritional needs. The great thing is that you can actually create a Do – It – Yourself gut load that contains the needed nutrients for your pet at home. It's very easy to make and quite inexpensive.

Here are the following tips on how to create your own gut load:

- Get at least two or three options (either fruits or vegetables) from the store in which you can use as gut

Chapter Five: Feeding Your Dwarf Caimans

load to your dwarf caiman's food, and then just rotate them every now and then.

- Always wash all the produce to rinse off any pesticide or chemical residues; peel the fruit's skin cover or cut the veggies because sometimes the pesticide or chemical components stick to the fruit or vegetable.

Gut – loading Ingredients

The following suggested ingredients should be the primary component of your gut load. They are high in calcium, low in oxalates, phosphorus, and goitrogens which is perfect for reptiles.

- Mustard greens
- Dandelion leaves
- Turnip Greens
- Collard Greens
- Papaya
- Escarole Lettuce
- Watercress
- Alfalfa
- Sweet Potato
- Carrots
- Butternut
- Mango
- Orange

Chapter Five: Feeding Your Dwarf Caimans

- Kale
- Apples
- Squash
- Beet Greens
- Bok Choy
- Blackberries
- Green beans

Toxic Gut – loading Ingredients

The following suggested ingredients should be avoided and must not be included in your gut - load. They are very low in calcium, and high in phosphorus, oxalates, and goitrogens.

- Cabbage
- Potatoes
- Iceberg Lettuce
- Romain Lettuce
- Spinach
- Broccoli
- Tomatoes
- Grains
- Corns
- Vertebrates (pinkies, lizards etc.)
- Oats
- Beans
- Meat
- Eggs
- Cereals
- Cat food/ Dog Food
- Fish food
- Canned/ dead insects

Supplementation

Calcium is very important to your dwarf caiman crocodilian's diet as well as vitamins that can be found in powdered supplements. You should sprinkle a small amount of these powdered supplements in the preys before giving them to your dwarf caiman. Use calcium twice a week, as well as calcium with D3 and a multivitamin at least once a month.

Feeding Tips

Below are some feeding tips you can easily follow and implement when feeding your dwarf caimans:

- If you are hand feeding your crocodilian, you better be careful because they usually tend to jump on their food. Your hand is vulnerable that's why it is highly recommended that you use a tong or anything similar that could protect you.

- Just leave the food on the dry area or on a dish if it is chopped. You can also put it in water but it could be difficult to clean since it will totally make a mess.

Chapter Five: Feeding Your Dwarf Caiman

- Sometimes, dwarf caimans are so shy and cautious that they won't touch their food until you are out of sight, if that's the case, just leave the prey and do not attempt to directly feed them or wait for them to grab it from you (because your hand is also a meal to them) especially when they are older, bolder and bigger already.

- Make sure to wash your hands before and after feeding to prevent transmission of diseases.

Chapter Five: Feeding Your Dwarf Caiman

Chapter Six: Dwarf Caiman Husbandry

After reading the previous chapters, you have already an idea on how to build a cage, the materials needed for an enclosure, as well as the equipment that need to be installed, this time you will be given in depth and technical information on how to keep your dwarf caimans happy while it is inside its habitat. You will learn husbandry tips including the proper amount of lighting, setting up the heat temperature as well as adjusting levels of humidity. This will help maintain a good environmental condition for your crocodilian.

Chapter Six: Dwarf Caiman Husbandry

Temperature

As mentioned earlier, crocodilians in general are semi – aquatic or semi – tropical species, that's why they are generally used to warm temperatures but some of them can also tolerate cooler temperatures. The ideal body temperature for dwarf caimans should be 19 to 34 degrees Celsius or 84 to 93 degrees Fahrenheit. During night time, it could drop to 20 degrees Celsius or 68 degrees Fahrenheit.

The water temperature should always be constant. The ideal temperature is between 27 to 31 degrees Celsius or 81 to 88 degrees Fahrenheit.

Humidity

Another important aspect of dwarf caiman husbandry is the humidity. Dwarf caimans can tolerate moderate to high humidity. The air temperature inside the enclosure highly depends on the room or location of where the cage is, if the room is too cold, the air heater should be set at a much warmer temperature and vice - versa.

You have to always make sure that the humidity inside the enclosure is just set at a right temperature to ensure that the humidity level is just right, you can use some form of

Chapter Six: Dwarf Caiman Husbandry

ventilation by providing a small fan, similar to a computer fan inside the CPU so that the air can properly circulate around the cage. However, keep in mind that the fan must not be too powerful otherwise it could mess up with other equipment.

Proper ventilation will provide a good airflow around the enclosure which will help in reducing fungal growth, and making sure that the enclosure will not overheat especially during summer or hot days. A good airflow will also benefit the growth of live plants inside the terrarium.

Lighting

As mentioned in the previous chapters, lighting is needed because even if dwarf caimans need sunlight to harness Vitamin D. Of course you can't just leave the enclosure outside so that your pet could get an authentic sunlight, that's why you will need to purchase and install a UVB bulb, incandescent bulbs or fluorescent tubes. The bulbs are usually good for only 6 months after which it needs to be replaced.

You might also need a basking bulb for your dwarf caiman. This bulb acts as a heat gradient that will allow your cold – blooded crocodilian to be able to regulate its body temperature. Switch the light on for about 11 – 13 hours

Chapter Six: Dwarf Caiman Husbandry

every day to resemble the sun during day time. You can also try dim light at night.

Just make sure that it doesn't exceed 26C (80F) degrees. Keep in mind that the UVB light must be on for about 12 hours, and also provide 12 hours of darkness inside the cage so that your dwarf caiman can rest. It will serve as their day and night period.

Chapter Seven: Handling Your Dwarf Caiman

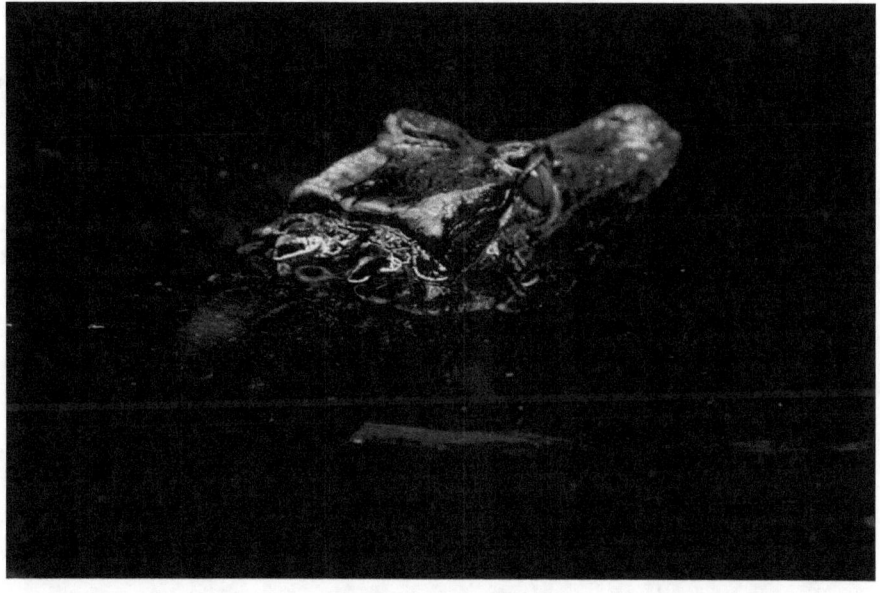

Dwarf caiman crocodilian and reptiles in general are observation pets which mean that they should just stay inside their enclosures for viewing purposes only. However, since you are the owner or care taker of this awesome creature, I'm sure one way or another you will need to hold them whether you like it or not. Such instance is when you clean their enclosures which mean that you must be able to handle them and take them away while you are cleaning their cage. You'll need to also feed them which mean that you'll risk your hand in getting bitten at some point, but then again it is part of keeping this kind of animal. The point is that one way or another you'll need to

Chapter Seven: Handling Your Dwarf Caiman

come in close contact with your pet, and if you're afraid to handle them, you should not be keeping them in the first place.

In this chapter we'll teach you some basic skills you need to know in order to properly handle your pet dwarf caiman so that you and your croc can get used to the idea of touching each other!

Basics in Handling Your Dwarf Caiman

As mentioned earlier, you need to know at least the basics on how to properly handle your pet crocodilian. However, for some owners, especially for people who just acquired this creature primarily for display or observation, they don't feel the need in learning how to handle their pet properly and because they believed that reptiles like the dwarf caiman should not be handled as much as possible due to the fact that these animals get stressed if they're constantly being handled. If they get stressed, it will be hard to feed them.

Other dwarf caiman croc owners completely disagree with the idea of "not handling" these creatures, because for them it's better for the dwarf caiman to get used to being

Chapter Seven: Handling Your Dwarf Caiman

handled or touch especially when they're still young for the very reason of not getting stressed out in the long run.

Aside from that, it's also beneficial to you as the keeper because if your pet has gotten used to being handled, the caiman will be calmer and it would decrease the chances of biting someone out of fear.

If you believe in the latter idea, then you should start handling your dwarf caiman at a very young age. It may not be wise to handle them when they're older because it will be increasingly difficult to make any impression as they grow larger, unless you already have an experience with such creatures.

Before learning some methods on how to handle your dwarf caiman you should learn some basic things about their behavior as soon as they get picked up.

Young dwarf caimans or most crocodilian species will regard your attempt in handling them as a threat. You and your hand will signal their brains out that a predator is here to eat them. You might hear an "eeow" kind of sound which means "help," in the crocodilian world. It's a distress call for these animals but once they recognize that they are being handled often, they will most likely habituate your presence and think that being handled is not a prelude to

Chapter Seven: Handling Your Dwarf Caiman

getting eaten. When you begin to consistently handle them and spend time around them they'll start becoming calmer and might be less inclined to bite although you still need to be careful and never let your guard down because crocs never will!

There's a possibility that your dwarf caiman can become relatively tame after a year or so but of course similar to most animals, their temperaments would vary. They can still mistake your hand for food so always be vigilant especially during feeding time. You can try picking them up at least once a day for several minutes; though you should keep in mind the environmental conditions because they could get stress if the temperature is too cold outside their enclosure. Observe their behavior and eating habit after you've handled them and adjust accordingly.

Handling your dwarf caiman at an early age can be a major advantage whenever you are cleaning its cage. Your pet will be less stress and possibly calmer whenever you interact with it but always keep in mind what these crocodilians are capable of especially when they grow older and larger.

Chapter Seven: Handling Your Dwarf Caiman

Tips in Picking – Up and Handling a Dwarf Caiman

For hatchlings or juveniles:

- For hatchlings or small dwarf caimans, pick them up gently from underneath and carefully lift them while gently straining their belly within the palm of your hand.

- Place your thumb over a front leg or on the base of its tail so that it can be restrained without restricting its movements.

- If your young dwarf caiman is trying to bite you, just place a gentle grip over their shoulders and neck using your forefinger and thumb so that it could prevent their small heads from turning and biting you.

- Don't panic or throw them away if in case things gets out of hand because they will get stress and will have more desire to bite you.

- For some owners it's better to start picking them up on the side so that the dwarf caiman can see your hand unlike handling them above (which resembles a

Chapter Seven: Handling Your Dwarf Caiman

predator attack). They could get used to it once they recognized that your hand is not a threat.

For larger or older dwarf caimans:

- Be extra careful because if you approach and try to pick them up from the side the way you do with a hatchling they could easily sideswipe their heads and bit you.

- Try to use a special catching noose because it's the safest way to catching and also restraining an older crocodilian.

- Relatively small dwarf caimans can be held in one arm. You should be able to support its body with your arm and you must pin its tail in your body to prevent it from struggling.

- If your pet is quite large, then you should firmly hold its neck and shoulders with one hand while your other hand should hold the base of its tail. Make sure to secure its tail against your body to prevent the animal from rolling.

Chapter Seven: Handling Your Dwarf Caiman

- If it tries to roll around, make sure to put firmer pressure around its neck because they are quite flexible and can easily sideswipe their head, be careful on where you put your fingers.

- Make sure to also support their pelvis and hold them comfortably, if they are comfortable it will settle down and not try to bite you.

- Never grab them by the tail because they can easily snap and crack your fingers open.

Important Reminders:

- Before you release or let go of your pet after handling them, make sure that their jaws are away from you or you set them towards the water where they could swim away. Don't give them the time to turn their heads and bite you once you release them. They are swift and lightning fast. Their powerful strike can surely wound you.

- You can secure its jaws by putting a duct tape or an adhesive tape and tying it around with a rubber band for added security (not too tight though, just make

Chapter Seven: Handling Your Dwarf Caiman

sure that even if the jaw starts to retract, the opening is not wide enough to slip a finger inside).

- Some people use gloves for added protection but some owner prefer not to because you may not be able to handle the dwarf caiman well. However, it's up to you if you wanted to use gloves or not.

Chapter Eight:

Breeding Your Dwarf Caiman

If keeping a Dwarf Caiman is already challenging enough for you especially for first time crocodilian owners, you might just want to stick to becoming an expert at it for a while before deciding to breed more of them. This chapter may not be suitable for everyone, even if you are already a long – time crocodilian owner. Handling and breeding female dwarf caimans can be quite challenging and it can take much of your time. Breeding can be difficult because these creatures are quite delicate and very sensitive,

Chapter Eight: Breeding Your Dwarf Caiman

however if you think you're up for the challenge, or would just want to know how breeding works, the information in this chapter can be useful for you. Read on!

Breeding Basics

Before you breed your dwarf caimans, it's important to note that you start breeding them when they are about a few weeks old already, according to some scientists, you can breed them as early as a day old, but that may not be advisable to every species.

If you are breeding a young dwarf caiman, it will be quite difficult to identify their sex, simply because they're still small. If you're not an expert, you won't be able to identify if your crocodilian is a male or female. Some owners mistake their female pet as a male pet because of very similar qualities in their pelvic area. Males exhibit a penis while female crocs exhibit a clitoris. Experts can also identify which is which by through various factors such as the body structure, the size or the shape of the crocodilian's vent.

If this is your first time breeding, you may need to learn from the experts. For you to be able to identify the sex of your dwarf caiman, you should do either of the following

Chapter Eight: Breeding Your Dwarf Caiman

methods: the popping method and the spreading the vent method.

- **Popping Method**

The popping method is usually used for hatchlings or very young dwarf caimans; if your pet is older it may not work anymore. All you have to do is to put firm pressure on the side of your pet's tail so that the penis could literally pop out (if it's a male). If no penis pop out, then it's a female obviously. You have to be gentle and not put excessive amounts of pressure otherwise you could injure your crocodilian. Sometimes the penis may be small and it may appear as a clitoris therefore mistaking it as a female. Sometimes it's the other way around, the females have large clitoris that when you pop it out it looks like a penis. You may want to go to the vet to make sure of its gender.

- **Spreading the Vent Method**

This method is quite tricky and you may need someone to help you hold down your croc to ensure that he/she will not struggle. You need to use forceps or a haemostat (or something similar) for you to be able to open its vent to reveal its cloaca.

Chapter Eight: Breeding Your Dwarf Caiman

You may want to pour a bit of water or oil on its vent opening so that once you insert the forceps it could get in easily. Once you got your forceps in your pet's vent, slowly and gently spread it. You are looking for a small and V – shape organ called cliteropenis (it's a term use for both male and female reproductive system because it is relatively similar in appearance.

If the cliteropenis has larger, longer, rounded and more tubular head that means your pet is a male species. If your dwarf caiman is a female, the structure will have a more triangular base and nothing is protruding compared to the male penis. This can be quite difficult especially for inexperience keepers. It's highly recommended that you just try the popping method.

Once you identify your dwarf caiman's sex, it's now time to mate them. You can place a male and female dwarf caiman inside an enclosure and let their natural instincts do its magic.

Nesting Baby Dwarf Caimans

Nesting for dwarf caimans usually occur between August to November, although for some species it occurs around April to August. Once your female dwarf caiman laid its eggs (usually in the water), it will then start

Chapter Eight: Breeding Your Dwarf Caiman

incubation. This is where you aid your pet during nesting. The temperature should be between 29 – 31°C. Its incubation period usually lasts for about 114 – 118 days, for some species it only takes about 100 days. The eggs are usually coated with a sticky substance. The male parent or the father usually cracks it open because the eggs are encased in hard excrement.

Hatching

After 7 days or more than a week, the eggs will start to hatch. In the wild, females usually lay just 5 – 9 or more eggs. The size of the egg for captive breeds is usually measures about 6.5 x 4.2 cm or larger, it's quite oblong in shape and weighs between 66 – 73 grams. The hatchlings measures about 23 cm long with a weight of about 43 – 47 grams. The egg mortality rate is low among caiman crocodilians which mean that it's very rare for newborns to die after hatching. Follow the feeding amount found in Chapter 5 once the newborn starts to grow.

Chapter Eight: Breeding Your Dwarf Caiman

Chapter Nine: Keeping Your Dwarf Caiman Healthy

Once you've bought a healthy dwarf caiman, you must know how to keep it healthy. What do they need? How much should you feed them? What are the symptoms of possible diseases? You should be able to tell when your crocodilian needs a trip to the vet. In this chapter, you will be given information about the potential illnesses that could threaten your dwarf caiman's health. Having an idea and information about these diseases can make you be aware of its potential threats and be able to prevent it before it affects your pet croc.

Chapter Nine: Keeping Your Dwarf Caiman Healthy

Common Health Problems

Dwarf caimans can be affected by a number of different health problems, even though crocodilians are healthy in general, they could still get stress, may inherit an illness from their parents and some of them are just pre – disposed to certain diseases due to many factors, which are generally not specific to any particular breed. Feeding your dwarf caimans a nutritious diet will go a long way in securing his total health and well -being, but sometimes crocs get ill anyway. If you want to make sure that your reptile gets the treatment he needs as quickly as possible you need to learn how to identify the symptoms of disease. These symptoms are not always obvious either; your dwarf caimans may not show any outward signs of illness except for a subtle change in behavior. As mentioned many times before in previous chapters, dwarf caimans do not show any physical signs and if they do, it's hardly noticeable.

The more time you spend with your pet croc, the more you will come to understand its behavior – this is the key to catching health problems early. At the first sign that something is wrong with your pet you should take inventory of his symptoms – both physical and behavioral – so you can relay them to your veterinarian who will then make a diagnosis and prescribe a course of treatment. The sooner you identify these symptoms, the sooner your vet can

Chapter Nine: Keeping Your Dwarf Caiman Healthy

take action and the more likely your dwarf caiman will be able to make a full recovery.

Dwarf caimans can be prone to a wide variety of different diseases or infections, though some are more common than others. For the benefit your crocodilian's long-term health, take the time to learn the causes, symptoms, and treatment options for some of the most common health problems.

Aside from red flags, it is best to be in the know when it comes to what these red flags mean. Dwarf caimans usually suffer from various common health issues you can find by identifying its symptoms or causes. Here are some of the common health issues to look out for:

Metabolic Bone Disease (MBD)

The Metabolic Bone Disease is the most common disease among reptiles in general. This disease is caused by a lack in dietary calcium, improper lighting, and also imbalanced nutrition.

As mentioned earlier in the feeding chapter of the book, your dwarf caiman should have the right amount of calcium and must eat food that is low in phosphorous. If the calcium levels are low, the body will be forced to get calcium source straight from the bones so that there will be

Chapter Nine: Keeping Your Dwarf Caiman Healthy

enough energy for the body to function especially for muscle movements and metabolism. The effect however is that the bones becomes weak and eventually brittle. This disease is very painful and definitely fatal for your crocs.

The usual signs you should look out for is bent leg bones, double elbows, stunted growth, decrease in the use of its tongue, double knees, misaligned mouth, soft jaw or if you it grabbing its own limbs or head.

If your dwarf caiman gets affected with MBD it cannot be reversed but the good news is that the process of progression of the disease can be stopped. If prevented, the bones can be treated with proper medications, and it can heal over time. Proper husbandry such as enough access to UVB lighting as well as proper nutrition can correct the calcium imbalance in the body. This is why bringing your croc to the vet once you see any early signs of Metabolic Bone Disease can be very helpful and lifesaving; it can stop further bone damage.

Intestinal Parasites

Intestinal parasites are composed of microscopic worms and protozoa that basically live inside you dwarf caiman's intestine. These kinds of parasites are very common among captive bred crocodilians.

Chapter Nine: Keeping Your Dwarf Caiman Healthy

Intestinal parasites are usually acquired from ingesting an infected or contaminated feeder as well as infected feces from other animals. The usual signs of intestinal parasites are smelly feces, lethargy, weight loss and lack of appetite as well as vomiting.

These parasites are microscopic and therefore can't be seen by the naked eye, that's why you need to bring in a fresh fecal sample for laboratory analysis. Usually deworming medications are prescribed but it's not a one – size – fit – all, it still depends on the kind of parasite living inside your pet. A fecal sample is taken to find eggs of the parasites, however sometimes worms are don't shed eggs so a negative fecal test doesn't necessarily mean that your pet is free from parasites. Several fecal tests or samples should be submitted.

Gout / Swelling Joint

If you've seen the joints or legs of your dwarf caiman swelling, it's an indicator that he has developed gout. Gout is a very common illness among reptiles. Its main cause is excessive uric acid that is found in bloodstream. If there is too much uric acid, it usually develops into a salt crystal which then builds up in your crocodilian's joint.

Chapter Nine: Keeping Your Dwarf Caiman Healthy

There are two kinds of gout:

- Primary Gout – usually it is caused by too much dietary protein
- Secondary Gout – it is caused by renal dysfunction among crocs. It is the most common type of gout among these creatures.

Unfortunately, this condition cannot be treated; medications can only alleviate the pain but not necessarily stop it. You can however prevent it through proper husbandry, it is always the best defense against diseases; if the environment or the enclosure is always clean it can ultimately help your dwarf caiman to have a healthy body.

The swelling of its joints is the result of the infected area inside the limb. A fluid sample may need to be given for laboratory analysis, and antibiotics should be taken. Your vet may also suggest cleaning or removing the affected joint to prevent it from spreading from other limb parts.

Stomatitis

Stomatitis, also referred to as Mouth Rot is a systemic infection. You will see a yellowish pus or discharge in your dwarf caiman's mouth if he has a stomatitis. Other signs of

Chapter Nine: Keeping Your Dwarf Caiman Healthy

mouth rot that you need to watch out for include blackening of teeth, and swelling of the lips or its jaws.

If it is not treated, the bacterial infection can progress and affect your crocodilian's jawbone as well as parts of its cranium which usually weakens the bones causing the teeth to become loose. It can also be potentially fatal. This illness needs vet treatment as soon as possible so that proper antibiotics and medication can be given, and so that the infected jaw can be cleaned.

Bacterial Infections

Like any other creatures, even humans for that matter are constantly exposed to bacterial infections. Thankfully, each of us – humans or animals have built – in immune system that fights the virus or bacteria that penetrate the body and protect it from further illnesses. However, in the case of reptiles, if your pet croc is stressed because of the environment or otherwise, its immune system can become weak which means that the bacteria can invade easily.

The main causes of bacterial infections are contaminated water, unregulated temperatures inside the closure or inappropriate handling and feeding, so to be able to prevent this, proper husbandry is the answer. You can reduce the stress by always making sure that you keep in mind your dwarf caiman's hygiene.

Chapter Nine: Keeping Your Dwarf Caiman Healthy

The most common signs include loss of appetite, listlessness, cloudy eyes, and redness on the underside of the belly and the thighs, as well as excessive skin sloughing with shed skin released in the water. Although symptoms vary, you should be able to spot one of these symptoms in your dwarf caiman. Extreme neurological or behavioral signs can also be noticed if the infection is not immediately prevented.

Make sure to bring your pet to the doctor so that your vet can prescribe the proper medications and treatment. Usually vets prescribe antibiotics to treat bacterial infections.

Obesity

Dwarf caimans are cannibals in general and they will literally eat anything, even animals that are bigger than them – even your hand! It doesn't mean though that they also require huge amount of food. You as the owner should still regulate their food intake to maintain a normal and healthy weight.

Some owners increase their croc's size through feeding the adult or mature crocodilians a similar feeding schedule of juveniles or young crocs which is more frequent than normal because they need more food for their growth. It's obviously inappropriate once your dwarf caiman already has a full meal. Others try to feed their caiman's with a prey

Chapter Nine: Keeping Your Dwarf Caiman Healthy

that is larger than their pet's size which could also pose a threat to its overall health.

Dwarf caimans can quickly reach its full adult size in a few months; once they reached their full – size most of the food they consume will be converted to fat and not so much use for the muscle or bone building because they're already passed that stage. As a result, the croc will become obese, which could also lead to a shortened lifespan.

For you to prevent obesity follow this feeding schedule for your frog:

- **Hatchlings or Juvenile Dwarf Caiman**: Feed it at least thrice a week or more depending on the meal size. Make sure to not give them food that are bigger than them to avoid digestive problems.

- **Adult Dwarf Caiman**: Feed it at least once or twice a week depending on the meal size. The amount may be larger since the frequency is much less.

Chapter Nine: Keeping Your Dwarf Caiman Healthy

Important Reminder

Dwarf Caiman Crocodilians can also suffer from different environmental stresses such as social stress, stress because of handling, feeding stress (due to improper feeding/schedule) and predation stress (if they are with another crocodilian). Make sure that you keep them happy and comfortable inside their enclosures and follow the tips mentioned in this book so that you can eliminate these potential factors. Most of the time the main causes of illnesses are improper handling, feeding and inadequate living condition, if you don't want any headaches in the future or expensive trip to the vets better invest your time in truly taking care of your pet's well – being.

Dwarf Caiman Care Sheet

Congratulate yourself! You are now on your way to becoming a very well-informed and pro-active dwarf caiman owner! Finishing this book is a huge milestone for you and your future or present pet croc, but before this ultimate guide comes to a conclusion, keep in mind the most important things you have acquired through reading this book. In the previous chapters, we have discussed the characteristics of a dwarf caiman, what it needs, the different tools you will need, the costs of keeping it, how to keep it healthy, and the proper breeding practice.

It may be a lot of information to take in, so we have compiled a care sheet to summarize the information you can find in this book.

Basic Information

Pedigree: evolved from archosaurs during the Triassic period

Breed Size: very small and has a relatively elongated body structure similar to a crocodile or an alligator

Length: adult length: 4 to 6 feet;
smallest possible size: 4 to 41/2 feet

Weight: around 6 to 7 kg or 13 to 15 pounds

Coat Texture: osteoderms, can also be smooth skinned, has thick and rough scales

Color: It has various shades of green, brown, yellow, blackish, fatigue color.

Patterns/Markings: It has various patterns resembling its natural habitat

Feet Type: birds, fish, reptiles and even large mammals

Temperament: shy, aggressive, quite dangerous

Strangers: may be threatened around strangers or if being handled too much.

Other Pets: Not advisable to introduce to neither other house pets nor the same breed. Keeping dwarf caimans in one enclosure is not a good idea.

Training: cannot be trained, but behavior can be quite predicted if the handler already has an experience

Exercise Needs: doesn't need exercise; recommended as an observation pet only

Health Conditions: generally healthy but predisposed to common illnesses such as parasites, hypoglycemia, and could also suffer from different kinds of stress such as thermal stress, capture stress or social stress

Lifespan: average 30 to 40 years

Habitat Requirements

- **Recommended Equipment:** Cage (wooden or glass), terrarium or enclosure, substrate, live and artificial plants, UVB/ UVA light, heat bulb, air and water heaters, gauges, gravel, stones, bowl dish

- **Recommended Day/Light Cycle:** 11 – 13 hours

- **Recommended Temperature:** 27 to 31 degrees Celsius or 81 to 88 degrees Fahrenheit

- **Recommended Humidity Levels:** moderate to high humidity

- **Cleaning Frequency:** clean at least once a day or every other day, regular spot cleaning.

Nutritional Needs

- **Primary Diet:** chicken, pork, beef, fish, insects, rat, mollusks, crustaceans, spiders, frog, lizards, small reptiles, small amphibians, small mammals and pelletized food.

- **Feeding Frequency:**

  Young and Juveniles: feed them thrice a week or once every two days

  Adults: feed them at least twice a week (depending on how large their previous meal is), adjust accordingly.

- **Primary gut – loading ingredients:** Turnip Greens, Collard Greens, Papaya, Escarole Lettuce, Watercress, Alfalfa, Mustard greens, Dandelion leaves, Sweet Potato, Carrots, Butternut, Mango, Orange, Kale, Apples, Squash, Beet Greens, Bok Choy, Blackberries, Green beans

- **Toxic gut – loading ingredients:** Cabbage, potatoes, Iceberg Lettuce, Romain Lettuce, Spinach, Broccoli, Tomatoes, Grains, Corns, Oats, Beans, Meat, Eggs, Cereals, Cat food/ Dog Food, Fish food, canned/ dead insects.

Breeding Information

- **Age of Sexual Maturity:** a few days or few weeks old
- **Number of eggs**: around 5 - 9 eggs or more
- **Incubation Period**: 100 – 118 days
- **Recommended Incubation Temperatures:** water: 25 – 27 degrees Celsius; Air: 26 - 28 degrees Celsius

Index

A

antibiotics 109. 110. 111. 112
appearance 3, 11, 15, 41, 111
attention 77, 78, 87

B

black 6, 8, 21, 116
body 6, 13, 14, 21, 22, 50, 70, 76, 77, 79, 80, 85, 90, 92, 110, 112
breeder 30, 37, 40, 41, 42, 43, 44, 45, 47, 48, 51, 53, 62, 86, 89, 92, 102
breeding 1, 10, 13, 15, 33, 41, 43, 85
brown 6, 29, 69, 116
brushy 24, 117

C

capable 7, 17, 22
captivity 6, 24, 32, 35, 63, 101, 103, 110,
captured 6, 17
care 1, 3, 5, 25, 28, 30, 36, 40
choosing 7, 40, 45, 62
colors 5, 6, 28, 41, 81
companion 7, 30, 121
contrasting 6
covers 8

D

dark 6, 21, 61, 65, 81, 105
delivery 17
diet 9, 42
different 5, 11, 21, 24, 31, 52, 65, 69
divided 17
docile 3, 5, 113
dusk 20

E

eggs 15, 21, 23, 24, 32, 73
embryo 22, 97
externally 21
eye 25, 59, 67, 76, 116

F

fact 15, 30, 32, 70, 73
family 14, 18, 20, 22
feature 17
feed 18, 27, 32, 37, 38
feet 14, 15, 32, 125
finish 18
found 14, 30, 31 33, 106
fun 82

G

generations 98

genes 21
gland 21, 24, 25, 116

H

home 59, 74, 104

I

illegally 15
interactions 15
interesting 15, 30

J

jail. 44

K

kick 13

L

large 14, 25, 26, 70, 73, 76
lid. 14, 97
little 13, 77, 78
live 71, 72, 73, 76, 77, 79

M

make	101
melanin	17
modified	17, 21
mouth	18, 23, 26

N

natured	15
new	41, 63, 82
North	14, 33, 112,
novel	15

O

outline	16, 125

P

patterns	14, 15, 100
personalities	14
physical	19, 75
predators	16, 69, 84
prep	13
popular	14, 105, 108

R

requirements	36, 37, 39, 74, 104

S

sign 67, 115, 120
skilled 15

T

threatened 90, 92, 117

Photo Credits

Page 1 Photo by user Cloudtail the Snow Leopard via Flickr.com, https://www.flickr.com/photos/blacktigersdream/8752957182/

Page 19 Photo by user Joy VanBuhler via Flickr.com, https://www.flickr.com/photos/joyvanb/8500532649/

Page 30 Photo by user Amy the Nurse via Flickr.com, https://www.flickr.com/photos/amyashcraft/2636693542/

Page 44 Photo by user Roni via Flickr.com, https://www.flickr.com/photos/roniweb/5310320225/

Page 59 Photo by user Roni via Flickr.com, https://www.flickr.com/photos/roniweb/5310909892/

Page 69 Photo by user trpnblies7 via Flickr.com, https://www.flickr.com/photos/trpnblies7/5795460946/

Page 78 Photo by user Allan Hopkins via Flickr.com, https://www.flickr.com/photos/hoppy1951/8290549855/

Page 82 Photo by user brx0 via Flickr.com, https://www.flickr.com/photos/atul666/4527684166/

Page 91 Photo by user Josh More via Flickr.com, https://www.flickr.com/photos/guppiecat/8128616687/

Page 98 Photo by user nmkef via Flickr.com, https://www.flickr.com/photos/95952368@N07/15272431211/

Page 108 Photo by user Josh More via Flickr.com, https://www.flickr.com/photos/guppiecat/8128631523/

References

Caiman – Wikipedia.org
https://en.wikipedia.org/wiki/Caiman

Caiman Care – ExoticPetVet.com
http://www.exoticpetvet.com/caiman-care.html

Captive Care – Crocodilian.com
http://crocodilian.com/paleosuchus/captivecare.html

Crocodilian Captive Care F. A. Q. - Crocs as Pets - Crocodilian.com
http://crocodilian.com/crocfaq/faq-2.html

Crocodilian Captive Care F. A. Q. – Feeding - Crocodilian.com
http://crocodilian.com/crocfaq/faq-5.html

Crocodilian Captive Care F. A. Q. – Handling - Crocodilian.com
http://crocodilian.com/crocfaq/faq-6.html

Crocodilian Captive Care F. A. Q. – Health Care - Crocodilian.com
http://crocodilian.com/crocfaq/faq-7.html

Crocodilian Captive Care F. A. Q. – Housing Crocodilian.com
http://crocodilian.com/crocfaq/faq-4.html

Crocodilian Captive Care F. A. Q. – Introduction Crocodilian.com
http://crocodilian.com/crocfaq/faq-1.html

Crocodilian Captive Care F. A. Q. – Purchasing Crocodilian.com
http://crocodilian.com/crocfaq/faq-3.html

Glossary of Reptile Terms – Living Art Reptiles
http://livingartreptiles.tripod.com/id62.html

How Do You Sex a Crocodilian - Crocodilian.com
http://crocodilian.com/crocfaq/faq-8.html

Keeping Caimans – Reptile Expert UK
http://www.reptileexpert.co.uk/keeping-caimans.html

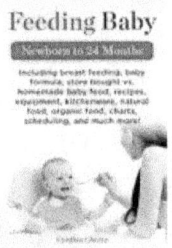

Feeding Baby
Cynthia Cherry
978-1941070000

Axolotl
Lolly Brown
978-0989658430

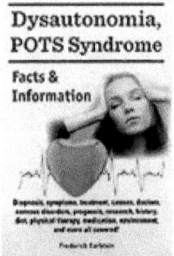

Dysautonomia, POTS Syndrome
Frederick Earlstein
978-0989658485

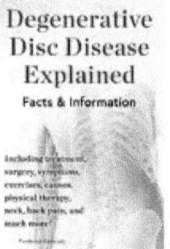

Degenerative Disc Disease Explained
Frederick Earlstein
978-0989658485

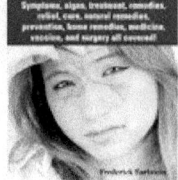

Sinusitis, Hay Fever,
Allergic Rhinitis Explained
Frederick Earlstein
978-1941070024

Wicca
Riley Star
978-1941070130

Zombie Apocalypse
Rex Cutty
978-1941070154

Capybara
Lolly Brown
978-1941070062

Eels As Pets
Lolly Brown
978-1941070167

Scabies and Lice Explained
Frederick Earlstein
978-1941070017

Saltwater Fish As Pets
Lolly Brown
978-0989658461

Torticollis Explained
Frederick Earlstein
978-1941070055

Kennel Cough
Lolly Brown
978-0989658409

Physiotherapist, Physical Therapist
Christopher Wright
978-0989658492

Rats, Mice, and Dormice As Pets
Lolly Brown
978-1941070079

Wallaby and Wallaroo Care
Lolly Brown
978-1941070031

Bodybuilding Supplements
Explained
Jon Shelton
978-1941070239

Demonology
Riley Star
978-19401070314

Pigeon Racing
Lolly Brown
978-1941070307

Dwarf Hamster
Lolly Brown
978-1941070390

Cryptozoology
Rex Cutty
978-1941070406

Eye Strain
Frederick Earlstein
978-1941070369

Inez The Miniature Elephant
Asher Ray
978-1941070353

Vampire Apocalypse
Rex Cutty
978-1941070321

www.ingramcontent.com/pod-product-compliance
Lightning Source LLC
LaVergne TN
LVHW051644080426
835511LV00016B/2489